AUTHORITY ISLAND

Why some authors become authorities and others just write books

Dixie Maria Carlton

— with Ann Dettori Wilson —

i.e.

First published 2020 by Dixie Maria Carlton

Produced by Indie Experts P/L, Australasia
indieexperts.com.au

Copyright © Dixie Maria Carlton 2020

The moral right of the author to be identified as the author of this work has been asserted.

All rights reserved. Except as permitted under the *Australian Copyright Act 1968*, no part of this publication may be reproduced, stored in a retrieval system, or transmitted in any form or by any means, electronic, mechanical, photocopying, recording or otherwise, without prior written permission from the publisher. All enquiries should be made to the author.

Every effort has been made to trace and acknowledge copyright material; should any infringement have occurred accidentally, the author tenders her apologies.

Product and other names used herein may be trademarks of their respective owners. The author disclaims any and all rights in those marks.

Cover design by Daniela Catucci @ Catucci Design
Edited by Lindsey Dawson
Internal design by Indie Experts
Typeset in 12/17 pt Garamond Premier Pro by Post Pre-press Group, Brisbane
Cover image by by Penny Hauck

 A catalogue record for this book is available from the National Library of Australia

ISBN 978-0-6487546-8-8 (paperback)
ISBN 978-0-6489310-0-3 (epub)
ISBN 978-0-6487546-9-5 (kindle)

Disclaimer:
Every effort has been made to ensure this book is as accurate and complete as possible. However, there may be mistakes both typographical and in content. Therefore, this book should be used as a general guide and is not the ultimate source of information contained herein. The author and publisher shall not be liable or responsible to any person or entity with respect to any loss or damage caused or alleged to have been caused directly or indirectly by the information contained in this book.

In loving memory of Wallace (Wally) Macdonald, an extraordinary man who seized life by the throat and could have filled thousands of pages about his many adventures and powerful lessons learned.

Contents

Foreword	ix
1: The Three Hopeful Authors	1
2: First, We'll Need a Ship	7
3: The Quest for Authority	13
4: Bob the Movie Star	25
5: Publishing 101	29
6: Never-ending Story	35
7: Owning Your Expertise on the Stage	37
8: Paparazzi by Any Other Name	45
9: Mastery of the Stage	49
10: Kris the Authority	55
11: Time to Set Sail	63
12: The View from Above	67
13: Bright, Shiny Objects	73
In Summary	85
Acknowledgements	91
Author Biographies	94

Foreword

Everyone wants to write a book – or so the experts say. Maybe not quite everyone, but most of those I meet are either already published, soon to be published, or want to one day be published. Every single one has a different story to tell and a different journey ahead of them as they set out to tell it. What really interests me is the variation in thinking, actions, and knowledge involved in the quest to become a published author. Let's be honest, anyone can do that nowadays, but the far bigger prize is to become an authority. An *author*-ity! An author who speaks, writes, shares, and teaches or inspires well beyond the words expressed in their book.

This story is one filled with many metaphors and wise ideas for authors of non-fiction, although fiction writers will also find a lot of these highly valuable. It is not my intention to teach the intricacies of how to do what's required to publish with this book, but rather to awaken authors to the reality sof just how much commitment it takes to succeed as an authority, not just a writer of books.

In my world, writing the book is just the beginning.

Dixie

1

The Three Hopeful Authors

'I've got the key to my castle in the air, but whether I can unlock the door remains to be seen.'
— LOUISA MAY ALCOTT, *LITTLE WOMEN*

This book is set out as a parable – a tale written to demonstrate important things that authors wanting to self-publish need to know. There's a big difference between just writing a book and becoming an authority who speaks, writes, trains, coaches or consults on a specialist topic. This book is not so much about writing well – although the better your manuscript is right from the start, the more likely it is to succeed – but about what can be done with any manuscript once it's finished. That's where your journey as an author really starts.

Let's begin our tale by meeting our three authors: Sue, Bob, and Kris. Come along with them as they head for a mythical place I call Authority Island – a land where, experiencing highs and lows, they can learn all they need to know.

Sue is a retired teacher who now spends a lot of time travelling, writing blog posts and helping others plan holidays. She wants to make a difference in the lives of people over 40 who want to have more meaning in their lives. Sue has travelled a lot, speaks several languages and studies something new every two or three years, just to keep her mind busy. Nearly 60, she has decided it's finally time to write the book she's been talking about for years.

As she sets out to become an author, Sue knows that first she just has to *write that book*. Then she'll get a friend from her school-teaching days to edit it for her, and then she'll find a publisher.

Sue's tool kit contains:

- ⚓ **A MAP** that she found by googling 'how to write and publish a non-fiction book'. It contains directions for finding Authority Island.
- ⚓ **A PEN** that she hopes to use one day for signing copies of her book, plus a laptop on which she will write it.
- ⚓ **A COMPASS** in the form of an accountability APP style of online program to help her stay on track with her writing. The program also comes with some optional half day 'How to Publish a Book' workshops to help authors work out what to do after writing a book.

Bob is a busy relationship coach who has already written a couple of books about divorce. Having dabbled with writing over the years, he has decided his words are worth sharing, his wisdom is well-founded, and he has quite a story to tell. He also has public speaking experience and has been told countless times that he really should write a book about how people's different personality types affect their relationships. As his regular blog is drawing social media followers – already in the hundreds – he figures there'll be good interest in what he wants to say, and so has decided that 'this is the year'.

Bob is unsure about self-publishing but was disappointed 10 years earlier by how his first book was handled by a well-known traditional publisher. It received very limited media exposure and scored few sales. Only a year after launch, his book was in the $1 clearance bin.

Bob wants his time and investment in the next book to be better rewarded. After writing his first draft and having it edited by a friend, he has decided to work with a company that helps authors like him publish a premium product – for a hefty fee. 'So, it better be worth it,' he grumbled when he paid the deposit.

Bob has similar tools to Sue:

- ⚓ A PEN, and also a MacBook Pro with extended battery life so he can write all day from the beach or the café across the road if he wants to.
- ⚓ A MAP for Authority Island. According to his costly advisors, it was verified and personally signed by a famous explorer named Indieauthor Jones.
- ⚓ A COMPASS in the form of a plan from the company

he's paying to produce his book and quickly push it to number-one status on Amazon.

Kris is determined to write a bestseller. She wants it to catapult her reputation as a specialist trainer in small-business strategy and leadership, and also to cement her status in the top echelon of speakers, writers and trailblazing experts in her field.

Kris's dream is to build a long waiting list of clients clamouring for her wisdom, all paying top-dollar for advice on how to rescue their businesses. Maybe she'll even have to turn work down if she gets too busy. Her ambition is to be booked solid for speaking gigs in far-off lands, flying Business Class and staying in good hotels. Her team at home will tend her clients well while she's away promoting her book(s) – surely there will be more than one!

Kris likes to back herself with support from top people. She has also invested in her own education, furthering her expertise, and knows the power of smart branding to command the higher fees she desires.

Kris has slightly different tools in her kit:

- ⚓ **A SELECTION OF WRITING TOOLS**, including a Montblanc pen and matching wristwatch, a MacBook Pro, a back-up laptop, and all the Bluetooth and Wi-Fi she could ever want for writing anywhere, anytime.
- ⚓ **A BOOK PLAN** she has constructed with the help of a highly recommended publishing coach.

⚓ **A COLLECTION OF RESOURCES** to help ensure she knows how to navigate the challenges and learning curves she's about to face. She wants no guesswork or delays.

Kris is ready to write a book series that changes the way leaders train their teams to do better and bigger business.

What our three hopeful authors have in common is a desire to share their words, wisdom and expertise to help their markets evolve, learn new things and take action. They share dreams of becoming bestselling experts, sitting on TV studio couches and being interviewed on the radio. What they don't know is that the work involved in becoming an author is very different from what it takes to become an authority in their respective fields.

But they are confident. After all, they've learnt a lot in their careers so far. Given the challenges each has overcome already, the idea of doing the hard work of writing a book seems relatively easy.

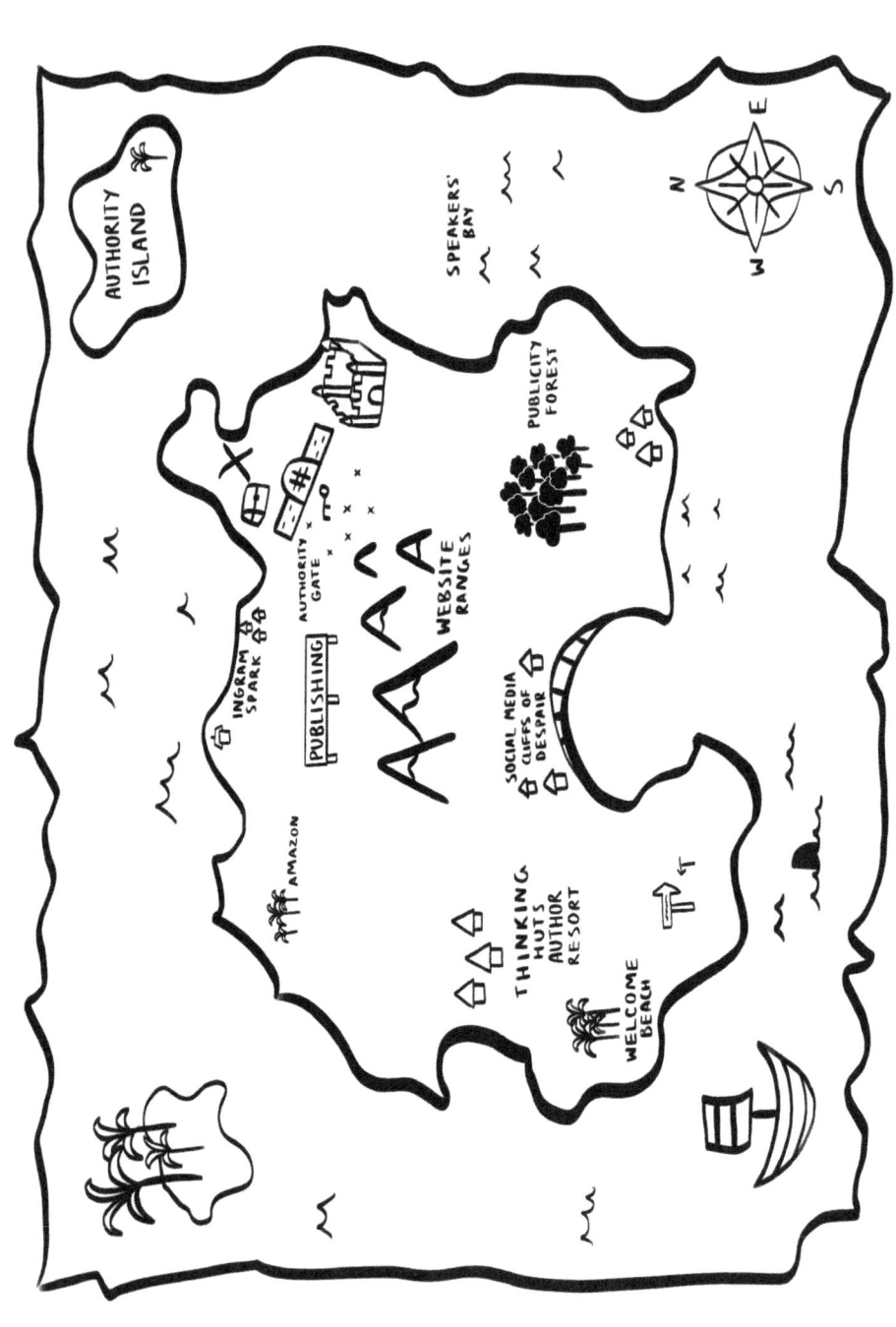

2

First, We'll Need a Ship

'Books are the treasured wealth of the world.'
HENRY DAVID THOREAU

You can't just fly into Authority Island. You might think you have seen enough YouTube videos to understand what it offers and even how to get there, but you still have to take the right journey and, once you arrive, find your way around.

Your ability to get attention for your book might be fast-tracked a little if any of these things happen to you: Your ability to get attention for your book might be fast-tracked a little if you've got a particularly dramatic or outlandish story behind you – or you're already a celebrity. But even with a ready-made spotlight, you will still have to do the hard yards of actually writing your story – yes, even if you're working with a ghost writer – and then go through the publishing journey.

THE IDEA OF JUST PICKING A TOPIC, WORKING UP SOME MATERIAL AND EARNING SWIFT CREDIBILITY AS AN EXPERT IS LAUGHABLE.

Yes, there's a lot more after that, and no-one is born just knowing how to do what comes next. That's partly because publicity and media, sales and distribution, and even publishing itself are constantly changing landscapes, but keep in mind that the people who need to read your book the most may never have heard of you. And they're not going to know you're available (and how very entertaining and clever you are) without some public relations effort and expertise. TED Talk organisers are not going to risk their brand by having you stammer your way through any variation of death by PowerPoint. You have work to do, my friend. Lots of it. Your book is only a part of the journey towards Authority Island.

Our three hopeful authors are hazy on how to get to Authority Island, but all soon discover they need a good boat. Sue wants to sail her own small catamaran, but Bob proposes, at the very least, a boat big enough to get through some rough seas if needed. Kris knows it is going to take a well-crewed launch, equipped with lifeboats for when things get rough, to get to her destination.

So how do they prepare? Before casting off and heading out, each of them loads up with necessary provisions. These include:

- ⚓ A completed 30,000-word manuscript that has been edited and proofed. Their respective files have been designed and formatted, and are ready to publish as soon as they reach Authority Island.

But let's explore what they've done so far in more detail.

Sue mapped out the outline of her book and then recorded her text. She then sent this voice recording off to a transcription service to be transformed into a written first draft. She read through the draft and made corrections, asked her old friend from the school English department to edit it. That friend did a good job of going over it, fixed lots of errors and suggested a few things that could add clarity to her message. Sue made additions, wrote an introduction and asked two people to review her book. They both did and offered further useful comments.

With her manuscript finished, Sue went to a book designer to order a cover design and checked that her Word document is properly prepared for turning into an Amazon-ready file[1].

Bob's manuscript is well-written and has already been edited by someone with wide book-publishing experience. She found errors, fixed them, and suggested ways in which he could rewrite a number of sections – and he did that so she could re-edit it, then proof the finished version.

His publishing advisors offered options for design and formatting and recommended a few things he'd not really thought

---

[1] Depending on whether you're uploading your book to Amazon as a Kindle ebook or a print book, you'll need different files. You can upload a .docx file directly for Kindle on Amazon, but not a PDF, whereas you can upload a properly sized PDF file onto Amazon for your print book version. However, there are other file versions to consider such as MOBI and EPUB, as well Amazon's own option for ebooks, KPF. Please always review Amazon and other platforms you want to upload to for their specific file requirements.

about, including adding a section outlining his availability as a consultant and speaker for conferences. They also advised him on what kind of files would be needed for uploading to Amazon and noted how vital it is for him to promote his book on his website and social media pages. They offered to introduce him to a marketing and publicity agent, but he decided to wait until after he's published his book.

The completed manuscript has also been reviewed by people familiar with Bob's field. They were very helpful and one of their comments is being used as a testimonial on the back cover.

The cover design and internal pages were done by book professionals who understand best practice and have ensured that the size is correct and ready for final-file creation.

Finally, Bob's manuscript was checked by a proof-reader for any additional last-minute corrections. Satisfied that his work looks really professional, Bob believes it's now time to publish. He is equipped with PDF files for uploading to both Amazon and print-on-demand company IngramSpark. He has also asked a local printer to run off a thousand copies.

Kris decided to take an easier approach to producing her book. Even before she started to write, she enlisted the help of a specialist *non-fiction* book publishing coach. Kris's manuscript is well-crafted and uses a tested method of structuring her information. She aims to follow the same plan to quickly turn out a second book within a year.

Following her coach's guidelines, she sent the draft manuscript to test readers. This process returned some insightful and very helpful comments. Kris was then able to finetune the manuscript to her high standards of satisfaction before a draft copy was delivered to an editor.

That editor was actually a *team* of three people who ensured that readability was outstanding, the error rate was almost nil and final proofing was done to the highest standards.

Once the final draft was signed off, the manuscript went on to a production team. The cover and internal design were crafted, and the pages typeset. The help of all these production specialists meant that the book was finished with important extras such as a dedicated sales page with calls to action. Additional design elements were also crafted for use on social media and websites, with a book information sheet for promotional use later.

Kris's files were provided in PDF, EPUB and MOBI formats, so that all variations required for uploading to a range of publishing platforms are taken care of. Her coach is also going to hold her hand through the rest of her publishing and *post*-publishing journey on Authority Island.

SOMETIMES WE GO THROUGH SOME PRETTY ROUGH SEAS TO HONE OUR SKILLS AND BE READY TO SHARE OUR EXPERTISE IN NAVIGATING THEM.

3

The Quest for Authority

You can't just leave school and get a degree in the business of professional expertise – yet!

– DIXIE CARLTON

Authority Island, as it's known in the experts' industry, looks from the outside to be a small and relatively exclusive place, as welcoming and well-appointed as any Caribbean or South Pacific oasis. You can't just drop in – some preparation is required and there's no landing strip for planes. There are beaches, a mountain range, and some clifftops. Of course, every industry has its own metaphorical version of a testing ground like this. It's not until you tie up your boat and step ashore that you realise you might have forgotten sunscreen, insect repellent and a hat.

Let's explore the journey taken by each of our three hopeful authors.

Sue arrives on the island having left her catamaran anchored off the reef. She has come ashore in an inflatable dinghy and is carrying a small case containing her manuscript and files. She breathes a big sigh of relief when her toes touch the sand and she takes a good look around. Her map has led her to the island, but she quickly realises she has no idea how to get beyond the welcome area. She locates a path that leads to a small group of buildings, the Thinking Huts Author Resort. She checks in and then finds the restaurant, where a small handful of authors is milling about. Taking a seat at the bar, she introduces herself to Dave the barman and orders a glass of sangria.

He hands her a welcome pack too, so she opens it and begins to read.

WELCOME TO AUTHORITY ISLAND.

Congratulations on writing your book! We hope you enjoy your publishing process. Here are a few tips to get you started. You are best to visit the various stops on the island in this order: Website Mountain, Social Media Cliffs of Despair, Publishing Platform Bays, Publicity Forest, and then finally to Speakers' Bay, where conference opportunities are held every month.

- To book your Website Mountain Guide, dial 1
- To book your accommodation at the Social Media Cliffs of Despair, dial 2
- For a map of the island and transport options, dial 3
- To order room service, dial 4

Collecting your mastery keys is the only way to gain access to the Authority Gate, so please do not venture there without those – you'll be turned back.

Enjoy your stay, and best of luck.

Management

'Authority Gate? Mastery keys? What are they?' Sue wonders aloud.

She folds the letter back into the pack and scans the brochures for the Social Media Cliffs of Despair, Publicity Forest and Publishing Platform Bays. But, tired now, Sue finishes her wine, orders a room-service sandwich, and books a guide for the morning to take her to Website Mountain.

The next day, with the help of her sturdy young mountain guide Mac, Sue discovers that Website Mountain is one large peak that extends into a formidable range. From a distance it looks relatively easy to climb. Though she has booked Mac's assistance, Sue is conscious of the fact that she feels quite capable of traversing the relatively easy pathways alone, and Mac's frequent stops at lookouts along the way feel like a relative waste of her time. Impatient to simply get going she decides push on by herself and asks Mac to wait as she forges her route alone. He tries to convince her of the risks of not sticking to the plan and pathways, but she is adamant that she doesn't really need him.

Mac finally gives up the argument and settles down to wait. He's met impatient do-it-yourself types before – mostly they think that taking shortcuts is justified and often like to prove their ability to save by not investing well in the things that matter because they simply can't see the real value in others' expertise. They often seem to need to fail a few times to fully appreciate the value of a higher quality option and good guidance, but they were also to be admired for their persistence, he felt.

Sue walks on, resting a few times, but the weather keeps changing and she doesn't have all the right gear or clothing to finish the journey. So, back down the hill she comes having not made it to the top to see the view of the rest of the island.

Mac smiles as she approaches. What Sue still hasn't realised, despite him trying to tell her, is that her website needs to promote both her book and herself as an author with a level of expertise her readers might want to tap into. The site doesn't have to be a huge investment, he says, but it needs to look sharp, well-designed, and be regularly updated so that when readers look her up she is well-profiled. And it needs to give readers a clear choice of ways they can order her book.

Not having all the resources needed for a full journey to the top of Website Mountain is an excuse many authors make. Of course, having a great website *can* end up just being an expensive indulgence. What Mac tries to communicate as they walk back to the Thinking Huts is that there are many options she can try.

Sue is a do-it-yourself fan who doesn't like paying for help from others. Her perspective is limited for now to only what she could see from the half-way point, but she had at least seen that the ranges went on for a long way to the east, with a lot of forest obscuring the land.

Arriving back at the Thinking Huts, she joins some other authors for a while. They're also new to the island and have spent the day in the Publicity Forest. Tales of giant spiders, wild pigs and quicksand are shared over a few beers. As Sue listens she decides to bypass the forest when it comes to that time in her journey, glad to be heading to the Publishing Platform Bays on the north coast the next day.

Behind the bar, Dave smiles at their chatter. He's been serving patrons here for several years now and has *seen 'em come and seen 'em go*. He knows the welcome pack specifically says the island's attractions should be visited in a particular order. But these authors seem to be pretty confident as they share ideas, so he is happy to let them be.

Dave is a veteran of the authoring game, having also once arrived with a manuscript, eager for fame and fortune. But when he nearly fell off the Social Media Cliffs of Despair and then saw tragic wrecks in Speakers' Bay, he retreated to the Author Thinking Huts for a bit of a re-think. Before long he found that bartending was a much easier option. He's delighted he still gets to meet so many interesting people. Plus, he has plenty of time to work on his sci-fi series.

Sue is undaunted. Despite the frustration she felt at the end of her first day and Mac's encouragement about exploring her options, she still feels she has committed enough time and effort already and won't abandon her dream. So she heads north. The first destination she finds is Amazon Bay, all set up with tents and Wi-Fi so she can get her book online. After a few hours figuring out the lie of the land, getting the hang of keyword searching and creating an author page, she feels ready to upload her ebook. Away she goes. It happens smoothly using a simple Word document. Thrilled with her progress, she then starts on her print book upload. That's when she hits her first major challenge.

Her files won't upload properly. The size of her PDF file keeps on being rejected, and the help desk is taking forever to be helpful. She paces up and down the beach as she waits for the process to go through its various stages. Other authors have set up camp around the bay and their stories make her more disheartened by the hour. Some of them have been waiting there for days for uploading and checking to be completed.

༺༻

TO OPTIMISE YOUR UPLOAD PROCESS FOR VARIOUS PUBLISHING PLATFORMS, YOU'LL NEED MORE THAN JUST WORD DOCUMENTS AND PDFS.

Deciding to cool down with a splash in the shallows, she spots a shark fin out in the bay and then squeaks 'Ouch!' as a jellyfish stings her shins. It seems Amazon Bay, so pretty and blue, is not as welcoming as it looks. Back up the beach she goes for yet another check of her files. They're still not loading well. Depressed, she decides to return to the Thinking Huts.

She finds Dave and cries out her frustration.

'I've come so far, and I'm so close …' she wails.

Dave pours her another sangria.

'Look, love, you can always just have your ebook up there, and still be an author. You still wrote a book and can use it to push your career along a bit further. You have options now. Option one is to leave it on Amazon but still head over to the Social Media Cliffs of Despair and learn what you can there. Then go on to Publicity Forest and get your media plan sorted. Your book might still give you the boost you want. Or, option two is that you could call your designer and see if he can fix the problem with your files. Wait here for a few days, learn a bit more about what else you need to be prepared for – or even go back home, redo your files, and come back next year. At least then you can return better prepared.'

Sue sniffs, takes a sip of her sangria and nods. Suddenly feeling woefully unprepared for all that lies ahead, she wonders if going home to learn more about what is needed to become an authority is indeed a better option for now. After all, she can still tell people her book was published on Amazon and that it still gave her some benefits with regards to her marketing.

Bob has also arrived at Authority Island. He stands on the beach, taking a long look at the boat he's left out at the reef, and the provisions he's brought ashore.

What a journey, he thinks. *I need a beer!*

He quickly finds his way to the Thinking Huts Author Resort and orders a pint from Dave. As he drinks it down, Dave welcomes him to the island, sharing a few of his own experiences and tales of other authors who've come to stay.

Bob learns eagerly about Website Mountain, the Social Media Cliffs of Despair, and the Publicity Forest. As he sets out next day for Website Mountain, he feels quietly confident that this part of the authority journey might even be the most *fun* part. After all, he knows he is a good climber, has already done some media interviews and has a great social media system run by his PA, Jane.

Bob is quick to appreciate the value of having a good Website Mountain guide. Mac is tough but firm in his advice that if you're going to make it to the peak, you have to have the right equipment, understand the weather, and be willing to hold on tight through any changes to the climbing plan. It isn't long before Bob realises that while he thought he was well-prepared for this part of the authority journey, his ideas have become outdated. In the last year, new climbing techniques and social media integrations have arrived and he needs to make some significant adaptations.

By the time he eventually gets to the top of Website Mountain he has spent more time and money than he meant to, but as he takes in the view of the whole island it is clear he's on the right track. Off in the distance he can see where the Authority Gate must be. Mac asked him when they started out that morning if he was collecting mastery keys, but Bob doesn't know much about them. When he returns to the bar that evening, he asks Dave what Mac was talking about.

Dave pours them both a shot of whisky and leans over the bar, playing with his glass before answering. Bob is one of the more serious authors he's met, and he's ready to share what he knows of the ways of the island.

'Well, legend has it that collecting all five mastery keys across the island grants you access to the area protected by the Authority Gate. Only with the mastery keys can you unlock the gate and become a *mega-successful authority*. But most give up before they even get there.'

'Oh,' replies Bob. 'No-one told me anything about collecting keys.' He pulls out his map, the one supposedly signed by famous explorer Indieauthor Jones.

'Nope', he says after studying it intently for a few minutes. 'Nothing about a key anywhere here.'

'Let's have a look at that map', Dave asks. Bob hands it across the bar, and Dave turns it upside down and over again before handing it back with a grin. 'How much did you pay for it?'

'A lot of money. I mean, more than I paid for my new car a couple of years earlier.' Bob is worried by the look on Dave's face, and his heart drops at the barman's next words.

'Mate, there is no Indieauthor Jones. Even the name is a joke – a play on a movie character. I should know. I've been here since 2008 when Amazon and ebooks were really starting to become a thing and IngramSpark arrived to set up along the bay a few miles away. I know for certain that there is no such person. Someone sure saw you coming and thought you looked like you might buy into the idea of a magic lamp.'

Bob's face is not one for poker, and his every thought is immediately written all over it. 'But can I still get there? I mean, can I still become an authority?'

'Sure you can! You just have to follow all the directions I give you.'

Dave, the bartender of 'Re-thinking Huts', who has never managed to get past the first part of his own quest for authority, settles in and proceeds to tell Bob, the author, how to gain access to the Authority Gate at the other end of the island.

'First you have to scale Website Mountain by proving that

you have your website profile all sorted and your basic branding looking *sharp*. Go and ask your guide for a key to prove you've already done that.

'Then to get your second key, social media presence, you have to demonstrate that you have all your social media running at a high level with *at least* hundreds of engaged followers. They form a big part of your launch plan. Your popularity is confirmed by how much engagement you get when you update your blog, post on social media, or publish a podcast episode. Getting onto other people's guest lists is also a good idea. This is all about social proof – ensuring that the market you are interested in is actually interested in you.

'Then you have to upload your files to Amazon as both ebook and print versions, create an author page, get more reviews, and then also add your book to as many other platforms as you can. IngramSpark and Draft2Digital offer lots of options for this, and their crews are pretty helpful if you get stuck. IngramSpark's print-on-demand option is brilliant and will save you the pain of buying stock you can't sell. That's a nightmare many authors are very familiar with: they order a tonne of books that end up gathering dust in the hall cupboard. Print on demand is a great way to avoid that particular trap.

'The next part of the journey is through Publicity Forest. To get your fourth key, your media skills need to be sharp so that your press releases get picked up, you score the interviews you want and start to enjoy some serious media attention. You'll probably need a whole lot of extra training to get that part right, or invest in a guide or PR agent. It's expensive, but sometimes they can get you a lot more opportunities. And it's still a lot less expensive than just endless advertising or "advertorials", which is where you pay for the privilege of having an article written about you or your book.

'Then you need to succeed in Speakers' Bay to get your fifth key. You have to know how to swim through the shipwrecks – plus there are sharks, fast talkers and snake oil salesmen to avoid. A lot of authors can't survive in this area and end up becoming just another wreck in the shallows. Now this part is the longest one. It will take time and coming back here each day won't be an option, so you have to commit.

'The best part is that while you're gaining experience you can meet and learn *from and with* other speakers and authors getting really good at this part of being an authority. It always surprises me that so many authors don't recognise the symbiotic relationship between the publishing and speaking industries. You will be hard pressed to succeed without being part of both. But Speakers' Bay is where you meet other authors and speakers, and form some lifelong industry friends and collaborators – your own tribe of associated experts.

'Everyone at Speakers' Bay is trying to make it as an authority, and you'll learn a lot of ways to build your ability to share your stories. You can get really good there. And a lot of authors start writing their next book while going through that training. It's a great place to connect with other speakers who also can teach you, learn with you and support your efforts.'

Bob is listening intently and writing down as much as he can, covering his now defunct *Indieauthor Jones* map with diagrams and scribbles.

'Once you have your five mastery keys, you can finally traverse the last of the mountain ranges. But be warned.' Dave downs the rest of his Glenfiddich before finishing, 'That is also the Bright Shiny Object Zone. By the time many authors and speakers get there, they are so bored by their own topic that they get distracted and want to change course. It's like sailing across the Pacific Ocean and being distracted by a pretty island with waving palms. You must stay focused and determined and sail past anything that might tempt you away from reaching your goal.'

Dave paused once again to top up both their glasses.

'By the time you get there you're so close you can almost taste the Authority Gate, so keep going.'

4

Bob the Movie Star

'What I like in a good author is not what he says, but what he whispers.'

— LOGAN PEARSALL SMITH

Back in his room that evening, after quickly collecting his first key from Mac, Bob looks for a long time at all the notes he's scribbled across his useless *Indieauthor Jones* map. Then he takes the proof copy of his book out of his case and studies the back cover.

He has put a lot into this thing and is proud of how it looks and feels. It's had some glowing early review comments. He knows it is going to boost his career significantly and will help a lot of people who read it. He is also conscious of how much money he's invested in it already. From what Dave has told him, there's still a lot more he'll need to pay out to become a recognised authority.

He decides he should contact his family. He needs to explain that his island stay will have to be a little longer than expected because the book still needs a lot of work.

'But I thought you already wrote it!' exclaims his daughter.

His wife is more sympathetic.

'I think you need to get the most out of the time you've already spent on it,' she says. 'Do what you have to do.'

He thanks her, ends the call and sighs. How long this might take he's unsure, but he knows he has to try.

The next day he heads to the Social Media Cliffs of Despair. The tents lined up along it are busy, and many other authors are also there to get their keys. It turns out the whole island is quite popular – and yet he'll soon find that the further east he goes, the more sparsely populated it becomes.

Auditors in the Twitter tent soon verify him as an authority because of his regular tweets and use of good images and links. His popularity is demonstrated by his several hundred active fans. He's heard he really needs to have above 1000 but is content for now with 964, and has promised to do what he can to increase the numbers. *At least*, he thinks, *I can be grateful that all of my followers are in fact genuine.*

It's the same when he gets to Instagram. Yes, his popularity is evident and his intelligent posting is quickly recognised. Having no food images is a bonus too – so many foodies on Instagram! – and his good mix of memes, with words and without, help enormously in revealing him to be a real person.

Facebook is almost an easy walkthrough until he is held up by failure in the advertising campaign zone. Assistants there show him again and again how to expand his audiences when boosting posts in order to thrive in the engagements index, but he can't quite get his head around it. Tired and fed up with the time it is taking, he finds some temporary accommodation on the outskirts of the cliffs and decides to tackle it again the next day.

The following morning dawns clear and bright, and he returns to the Facebook tent, eager to see if somehow the things he's been struggling have magically embedded themselves inside his brain. It takes a while, but by mid-afternoon he finally feels that he has mastered the process of boosting posts, targeting specific audiences, engaging with other groups, and increasing his reach enough to satisfy the auditors.

Finally, he can move onto LinkedIn. Mastery here is a totally different matter. For a start, it targets a different audience and is in many ways far more sophisticated. Bob believes his readers will most likely be more active on LinkedIn than on Facebook. He spends the next few hours learning about aspects of LinkedIn he never even knew existed. He creates a company page, increases his recommendations, both received and given, adds some of his articles and videos to his profile, and then learns about the different types of posts and articles he can share. Engaging with groups and commenting on other people's posts in a way that is genuine, consistent and actually enjoyable is also a bonus, and by the time he's finished he can truly value the comprehensive tool that LinkedIn is for authors like him.

His final hurdle, the Audio Visual Media tent, is the last of the long line, and from the outside looks to be the smallest. But stepping in through the flaps, he opens his eyes in wonder as the ceiling looks infinite. Sparkling stars shine down from above, making the room light and bright. Behind the front desk a hall of mirrors stretches away from his gaze, each surface showing a different scene. Videos play in loops, and at the far end of the hall is a door with a sign marked STUDIO on it.

Bewildered by how the tiny tent has become like a Tardis, increasing its size and capacity twenty-fold, Bob steps up to a large, old oak desk. A skinny, young geek looks up with a smile and hands him an iPad with a preloaded digital form to fill out.

And that's when it all falls apart.

Bob knows next to nothing about creating a YouTube channel or making videos, and certainly not much about how to manage his Google account – the prerequisite for success with YouTube. He fills in the form and has a brief but productive conversation with the geek in which he is asked to return the next day.

※

AN AUTHOR'S JOURNEY IS ONLY JUST STARTING ONCE THEY FINISH WRITING THEIR BOOK – GETTING LEVERAGE ON THEIR WISDOM IS WHERE THE REAL WORK BEGINS.

Over the following week he learns about creating videos for YouTube and Vimeo, selecting software for enhancing his look and sound, marrying up his video footage with audio tracks, cutting text and graphics into his movies, using Zoom and a variety of other tools to market his channel.

It's exhausting and he often wishes his PA was there too, but he realises that his to-do list must now include hiring a social media specialist to handle some of this for him in future. He battles on with the program and feels at the end that he has achieved more than he ever dreamed was possible when he began his book. He is brimming with ideas about turning its content into vlogs and even an online program or series of workshops.

5

Publishing 101

If you want to be a writer, you must do two things well above all others: read a lot and write a lot.

– STEPHEN KING

Bob is not done yet. He pauses at a crossroad, trying to decide what he needs to do next. If he takes the right fork, he'll end up in Speakers' Bay, which is closer than going all the way back around the Website Ranges to reach the publishing side of the island. The left also takes him back to the Thinking Huts.

He decides that after the rigors of the Social Media Cliffs of Despair and all the learning he's done that a rest back at the Thinking Huts would be time well spent, so, with a sigh, he picks up his pack, turns to the left and starts walking.

As he passes Website Mountain he thinks about how his new social media skills will enhance his website and is still smiling at the ideas crashing through his mind when he makes it back to the Thinking Huts.

Dave is tending bar and more authors have arrived. Bob joins them. Needing company as much as anything, he shares where he's been and some of what he's learned. The other authors are fascinated, and they all laugh over their shared experience of buying the *Indieauthor Jones* map.

'Someone's making good money off that scam,' pipes up one of the newbies.

Bob has Amazon Bay in mind the next morning and makes his way to the publishing area with his manuscript.

It takes only a few hours to make his way around the site, upload his ebook files, and then start on his printed book files. That goes well too. His files have been prepared well by his designer back home and so he can spend the afternoon checking keywords[2], revising his descriptions and categories with the help of an Amazon assistant, and then finishes the day by creating his author page.

The sun is just starting to set when he turns his computer off. Three other authors are sitting on the beach; they share their names – Harry, Frank and Jo. Someone's lit a small fire. Bob finds a seat on a log and listens to the conversation. They're debating whether to go wide or narrow, and Bob asks what that means. Jo, an older lady with tightly curled hair and a wide smile, explains that going wide means having your book on lots of platforms, versus going narrow by just sticking with Amazon and focusing all your marketing there.

---

2 Programs like KDP Rocket and other tools by Kindlepreneur are incredibly helpful for authors working through this stage of uploading their books. Please see the link at the back of this book for more details.

Frank and Harry sound intent on keeping things easy and sticking with one main platform.

'Then why, if you are only going to upload to Amazon, are you still here?' asks Bob.

'Because if we at least wait to check our files are ok tomorrow, then we don't have to come back,' says Harry. 'In the morning we'll log on and see if our books are live yet, and if so we'll move on to Publicity Forest. We're hoping that it's all pretty straightforward.'

Jo leans forward and shakes her head. 'You guys are crazy not going to IngramSpark first. The files you have can be uploaded there with only minor adjustments. You'll reach a much wider audience – after all, not everyone likes Amazon, and some readers really *prefer* Barnes & Noble or Book Depository. Why make it harder for your book to perform across multiple channels?'

'Because I'm happy with Kindle Direct Publishing. With KDP my book is promoted better by Amazon, and it's the third biggest search engine in the world so anyone looking for my topic is going to potentially find me and my work,' counters Harry.

'You see,' he adds, 'if I can totally ace it on Amazon with a good-build up to my official launch date, then I can promote my book, keep the pressure on via social media and send readers to one main link (that being my author page) where they can see options for which country to buy in, which version they want – ebook, print or even audio. It's easier than managing a lot of different platforms. Even the reporting and payment system is easier.'

Frank nods in agreement. 'Who has time for all the work involved in making your books go wide? I mean, the website, blog posts, social media, and podcasts are almost a full-time job as it is.

I'd rather do one part of this really well than split my focus across any more platforms.'

Jo shakes her head. 'You guys are wrong, and you're missing huge marketing potential by not having your book available everywhere. If you want bookstores to stock copies, and a print-on-demand alternative for when Amazon can't or won't supply to certain places around the world, then you have to upload to IngramSpark.'

Bob is keen to talk further with Jo in the morning. But for now, grabbing a sausage and some bread off the community BBQ, and finding a corner of the beach on which to curl up on a blanket is all his tired mind can handle.

In the morning, waking up to the sound of seagulls, Bob slowly rolls over on his sandy blanket and props himself up on his elbow. Waves are gently breaking a few meters away, and he's startled to spot a couple of shark fins circling near the squawking gulls. So much for an early-morning swim. Rolling up his blanket and dusting off sand, he strolls back up the beach to where the Amazon helpers are handing out coffee. Authors are crowding into the tent to check their files' status.

To his relief, Bob finds that his ebook and print files have been checked and cleared for take-off, and so his launch date is firmly confirmed – and with a marketing campaign in place including a countdown deal to ensure pre-sales he can move on to the IngramSpark tent further up the beach.

He is delighted to see Jo heading in the same direction, and he catches up to her and asks if she would mind expanding on what she said around the fire.

'Sure,' she says. 'I'd enjoy the company.'

As they stroll, she explains her thoughts about using other platforms. Bob's not even heard of some of them before.

'Draft2Digital enables your ebook to also be listed on Apple Books, NOOK, Kobo and a long list of other online retailers. You also want to be on Barnes & Noble, Book Depository, and Booktopia – their online and offline options are available by listing your book in ebook, audio and print form on a range of platforms including IngramSpark, Amazon, Draft2Digital, OverDrive (which is for libraries), and Findaway (which is for audiobook distribution). This way you get to promote more than just one option, which is typically on Amazon Kindle. Not everyone wants to download the Kindle reader, and not everyone wants to buy across multiple platforms overall, but a lot of readers do like that range of choices.

'You also want to know that if you want to send a bulk load of books anywhere, you can do it via IngramSpark's print on demand, which offers many more options than Amazon's own print-on-demand service. That said, all of these places are committed to making improvements all the time, so there's a bit of a risk because you're at the mercy of their changing systems.

'One of the new ideas around, called Publishing 3.0, is that very soon readers will be able to order a book from our websites in a way that bypasses all the platforms and sends copies to them directly via a print-on-demand service. This will give us authors more control over a lot of things, which is very exciting. For now, it's great we have so many ways to sell and for our readers to be able to get our books, but the publishing industry in general is becoming more complex and therefore more problematic for use to navigate.

'In a nutshell, we have to keep working at this and ensure our books are good enough – both in how they are written and how they are produced – to rise above all the rubbish that's on sale out there.'

Bob takes in all her comments and does his best to commit them to memory.

At the IngramSpark tent they join a short queue of other authors waiting to upload their files. A serious young man with tiny round glasses, wearing a fluoro-green t-shirt with a smiley under the words 'Ask me for help', is checking with each person whether they've completed their pre-upload work.

The forms he's referring to ask about their tax status in several different states of the USA. They also need to supply their book ISBNs, keywords, descriptions, author bio, contents information, reviews, and book categories. So long as they have all these things in hand, they can go smoothly to the upload stage with their files.

By the time Bob and Jo have finished it is well into the afternoon, so they decide to scout out some accommodation options for the night. They find the area is in fact a small village with several tents set up, much like on the Social Media side of the island.

The brightly signposted BookBub and Booksprout tents are easy to identify. BookFunnel is situated a little further way. Draft2Digital, Kobo, OverDrive and Findaway are next to the restaurant and bar, which in turn is next door to the hotel complex. All of these options represent various ways to get distribution and market books in all genres across a range of platforms.

After a swim and a shower, Bob meets Jo and some others they've gotten to know and together they find a long table for dinner.

6

Never-ending Story

"Bare lists of words are found suggestive to an imaginative and excited mind."

— RALPH WALDO EMERSON

Food arrives and conversation rolls on around the crowded table. Some authors have already been through the IngramSpark upload process, and can compare notes on whether it's easier or harder than Amazon. Others have tips to share on all the other publishing tents. New arrivals like Bob and Jo sit back and listen. As the alcohol flows and voices get louder, much of the post-midnight talk is lost in the sound of clinking glass and rising levels of laughter.

Bob has a lot to think about the next morning. He's learned so much more than he ever imagined he'd need to know. It feels like he's been away a long time, but he's still far from being good at this.

If only, he ponders, *I'd known a lot more before arriving on the island. That way I'd be feeling far more certain about how I can get a return on my investment of both time and money.*

Either it was a huge mistake to write the book at all, or he is about to step up to a whole new level of expertise and experience. He just isn't quite sure what the future really holds. Still in his pre-retirement years he's already done a lot of planning around surety of income, has implemented solid structure in his work life and has been seeing good outcomes for projects he undertakes. But authorship is beginning to feel like a boat bobbing about on a cold lake where one wrong move might spill him into icy water, offering little chance of survival.

He heads to the IngramSpark tent and sits in on a lecture for new authors. It's a couple of hours well spent, and he leaves with helpful handouts. But as soon as he steps outside, he is harassed by guides urging him to pay big money for advice on other publishing options. He decides to hoard his handouts and navigate his own way around, saving his money for the next stage of his journey.

Uploading his files to IngramSpark goes more easily than Amazon, and takes considerably less time. He is therefore able to work his way through several of the other tents, but by the time he returns to his lodgings he is feeling quite exhausted. Cramming such a lot of information into his brain is starting to take its toll.

So far, he has managed to collect mastery keys from Website Mountain, the Social Media Cliffs of Despair, and the Publishing Platform Bays – and he's about to face Speakers' Bay. He wonders how much longer this is all going to take.

7

Owning Your Expertise on the Stage

'Believe in yourself and readers will believe with you!'
— ADELE ROSE

Packing up in preparation for the next stage of his journey, Bob isn't too concerned about the demands of the Speakers' Bay program.

He's certainly done a lot of public speaking over the years in his work and even stepped into Toastmasters for a while to prepare for a series of wedding speeches in his 20s, so he's confident about talking to a crowd. Surely it couldn't be too hard to become a *professional* speaker considering he has a book to talk about on a subject he knows inside and out – and, he hopes, a willing audience for his particular topic?

He arrives at Speakers' Bay just in time for what appears to be a conference in its giant convention centre. Picking up a lanyard at the front desk, he moves with a small crowd into the conference room and finds a seat near the back.

The first speaker talks for exactly 45 minutes about leadership and receives resounding applause. Well-deserved, too, thinks Bob. He's eager to hear the next speaker, a woman whose topic is bullying. She uses powerful stories and just a few PowerPoint slides to push her message of curiosity and empathy as a means of overcoming bullying. Her personal insights and experiences move several people to tears and the audience gives her a standing ovation. Bob is further impressed by the next speaker, an entrepreneur named Steve who shares the story of how, after the dramatic failure of his business, he found a way by pivoting it from being a bricks-and-mortar company to an online service. Another standing ovation.

At lunchtime, Bob is delighted to find himself talking with Steve over salad and bread rolls.

༄

AUTHORITY IS NOT SOMETHING YOU CAN LEARN FROM ONLY READING BOOKS – YOU HAVE TO GET YOUR HANDS DIRTY, YOUR FEET WET, AND YOUR MIND OPEN WIDE TO ENDLESS POSSIBILITIES.

'You were great,' he says. 'What a story!'

'Thanks, I am glad you enjoyed it.'

When Steve asks Bob why he's at Speakers' Bay, Bob is only too pleased to talk about how he wants to use his book to become a recognised authority on relationships between managers and staff.

Steve nods. 'Do you have any special knowledge about that?'

'Yes, of course,' says Bob proudly. 'My work is all about helping to develop better teams in corporate business.'

Steve just smiles and lets him go on.

OWNING YOUR EXPERTISE ON THE STAGE

When he's finished, Bob is hoping for some enthusiasm to come back at him, but Steve simply leans in, claps him on the shoulder.

'Good luck, mate,' he says. 'You might want to check out the next speaker in particular. Abraham could be exactly who you need to hear from right now.' And then he disappears into the crowd.

Feeling a bit put out, Bob puts down his coffee cup. Who is this Abraham person anyway? He tucks in his shirt and smooths one of his eyebrows before heading back for the next session. Someone's already in the seat he'd used before, so he ends up close to the front of the room. Looking about, he notices an air of excitement. When the next speaker is announced many people stand up to welcome him onto the stage, clapping and cheering.

'You can't go there till you *grow* there!'

Abraham's opening line is powerful. He repeats it. Then looks at every person in the front row and slowly brings his hands together to rest comfortably in front of him. Pausing in front of Bob, he peers closer.

'I bet you, and everyone else in this room thinks that writing a book is all you need to do to become an authority in your field. To get on stage and become a hero to all the managers, coaches, trainers, and wannabes that ever lived in your mind and might need a shakeup. That your material is going to be "ultimately the most important thing they'll hear all year". He pauses again and looks towards the back of the room. 'Well I'm here to tell you you're wrong. That no-one gives a big rat's todoodle about what you have to say. No-one cares.' He paused to let that sink in. 'No-one cares about your "stuff" as much as you do, or maybe your mother. And you know why?'

He waits until someone yells out, 'Because they heard it all before?'

'Yes, but that's not it!' says Abraham with a smile.

'Your news is the same as someone else's, just packaged differently?' tries another hopeful voice.

'Yes ... but that's still not it.' Abraham is warming everyone up with his gentle but firm banter, charming smile and endearing shrugs. 'It's simply that you don't know how to deliver your stuff in a way that everyone finds interesting. You ain't figured out the best way to coat your facts in delicious, sugary, sticky, gooey stories. Because you know what?'

He pauses again and makes a summoning motion with both hands to the whole room ...

'What?' the room shouts back to him.

'Stories are what make the facts sticky. And you have to learn how to be a good storyteller to make people sit up and take notice of what you have to say. And you know what else?'

Again, the summoning gesture, this time with a cocked eyebrow.

'What else?'

'You can't go there till you *grow* there.'

Introduction over, Abraham explains for the next hour what makes a great presentation *truly great*: how to deliver your information in story form so that your audience, your readers, and your market will get it and remember it.

Bob has never seen a presenter so good at holding his audience in the palm of his hand, able to woo them with his voice, gesture with his whole body, *persuade* them to learn more. Looking around, he sees everyone is hanging on every word coming from the man's mouth. He's like a rock star who knows exactly when to hold a note, when to sway and when to stop abruptly before playing the next chord.

When it's over, Bob, like many others in the room, lines up to buy Abraham's books. All of them. Then with his mind reeling, he checks into his room and lies down to pick up the first book. It is midnight when he finally turns off his light, eyeballs scratchy with tiredness, but his mind still eager to absorb more.

Next morning, the breakfast room is buzzing with guests waiting to absorb what might yet be shared by the remaining speakers.

It's another long day of presenters. Some are outstanding, but some are very boring, sharing content of barely average quality. By 4pm the conference vibe is starting to dwindle. Yesterday's energy is fading, and people are starting to leave. By now, Bob is wondering, *Is this it?* Surely he won't be granted a Speakers' Bay mastery key after only listening to a bunch of good-to-great presenters.

Then a woman comes up to him and invites him into a side room with several other people. Her name tag says 'Sarah'.

'You may be wondering why you are here, and what happens next,' she says. 'Well, what you've just seen is a conference where highly certified, and in many instances award-winning, speakers have shown you all the difference between "public speaking" and "professional speaking".'

She pauses to let the distinction sink in.

'What you may not have been aware of when you arrived, or even when you began writing your books, is that just being able to stand before a crowd and talk is not enough to command the kind of authority you are all seeking as authors.

'Those of you who want to press on towards that lofty goal are now invited to sign up for the learning you need to do in order to become every bit as good or better than the worst of what you've seen today. And yes, there were definitely a handful of less-than-great presenters. They were there to ensure you could understand the difference.'

Sarah then outlines the entire speaker-training program to the people in the room. She also explains that the rest of the conference attendees have either already left to return to the Thinking Huts complex, or are trying to short-cut the program and would likely soon be making their way to the Publicity Forest's Media Training Centre with tales of being swept out past the wrecks in the bay having narrowly avoiding total annihilation, while a handful more are trekking back to the Social Media Cliffs of Despair to see if they can simply become 'online-only gurus'.

'Good luck to *them*' she says. 'Now, I propose you all get some dinner and talk with each other – a good tribe is important in any industry of experts. If you decide to sign up tonight, we'll meet back here in the morning for our first three days of speaker training. Then on Friday, we'll buss you all into the Publicity Forest to start learning more about media and publicity.'

Bob takes the plunge and tackles three days of intensive workshops. They include instruction on developing handouts, mastering advanced platform skills, setting appropriate fees, creating added value and building a powerful keynote that can be converted to breakout sessions and workshop material.

After all that, Bob has to admit that the speaking skills he'd thought of as being relatively easy part are in fact a lot more complex. The *business* of being a speaker on any specialist topic is far and away from just standing and talking about your subject in a 30–60-minute time slot.

Then it's onboard the bus and they're off for their media and publicity experience – another three-day program.

8

Paparazzi by Any Other Name

"If you would not be forgotten as soon as you are dead and rotten, either write things worth reading, or do things worth writing."

— BENJAMIN FRANKLIN

Arriving at the welcome desk at the Publicity Forest's Media Training Centre is quite a novel experience. For a start, the walls are lined with photos of famous novelists, as well as other great writers of historical dramas, plays and even poetry. The photos are cleverly arranged to inspire a closer look. Elizabeth Gilbert peers earnestly across the room, her gaze crossing paths with Seth Godin, who in turn is being looked up at by several presidents of the United States. Deepak Chopra looks amused by something Malcolm Gladwell may have said, and Stephen Covey is raising his eyebrows at Tony Robbins.

Bob would love to spend longer soaking it all in, but he and the team are ushered into a boardroom where coffee and dark-chocolate Tim Tams await. Seated at the head of a long table is a short, older lady. Yet another guide, yet another name tag, This one says 'Gerry'. She has crinkly grey eyes and a bright-pink mouth apparently set in a permanent scowl. She reminds him a lot of Dame Maggie Smith, and yet also a bit of his own mother. She taps her pencil impatiently on a legal pad as they all trail in and give her their names. Gerry writes them down alongside a brief description.

'You are here because you are authors, and each of you wants to become an *authority* in your field,' Gerry says. 'In order to do that you need to know a lot more than you thought you did a few weeks ago, but by now your brains are probably a little tired from all that you've had to cram in there, am I right?'

A couple of people in the room snicker nervously, perhaps unsure if she actually means to be amusing or not.

'I am here,' she announces, 'to instruct you on some simple ways you can get the attention of the media for your books, how to write half-decent press releases, where and how to send them out, and then what to do if any journalists, editors, producers or agents bother to pick up what you're putting down.

'If you have no boring or time-wasting questions let's get on with it, shall we? We'll thrash out a few things for the next hour or two, then I'll take you for a tour of the studios before lunch. This afternoon you'll experience what it's like to be interviewed by TV show hosts. Then we'll discuss ways you can get better at being brilliant at talking in sound bites.'

Sound bites is among Gerry's favourite phrases. She speaks them in crisp tones, emphasising each consonant as though she is teaching English to foreigners. Sound bites, she insists, are the mainstay of a good interview. Being able to talk in crisp, *memorable* sentences, answer questions in short *whole* sentences, and show interviewers you can perform well in any media situation is key to getting invited back.

'Practice your ability to speak in sound bites at every opportunity,' says Gerry. She makes them watch *Oprah*, *The Project*, and even *Jimmy Kimmel*, to see how each of them asks questions. 'That's how you can start to identify tricks they use to get you talking, and how you can get the most out of your time on air.'

Bob learns how to guard against being put on the spot by an aggressive questioner and how to respond to a producer calling to book an interview. He writes out and practices lines that encapsulate his most important points so as to ensure every moment on air is maximised. He also learns a little about how to dress so as to look his best on camera.

Three days later, they are done. Bob goes to his room and collapses on the bed, exhausted. Like most of his associates, he falls asleep before dinner, still fully dressed, thinking about the past week.

When in the morning they go back to reception to check out, there's one more form to sign. They've had publicity photos taken the day before, and they now give permission for their faces to be added to the crowd of photos on the walls – if and when they and their books become famous.

It's clear they still have some work to do before they reach that point, but Gerry wishes them all well as she farewells them at the bus, pressing their mastery keys into their hands along with a kiss on the cheek.

'We don't settle for a handshake when a hug will do,' she gushes.

It feels like being blessed by the Queen herself in some way, and the mood is jubilant all the way back to Speakers' Bay.

They all think returning there is simply a formality, that they'll collect their keys and then make their way to the end of the island where they can hand over *all* of their mastery keys and complete the launch of their books (and themselves) to the marketplace as bona fide authorities.

They are wrong.

9

Mastery of the Stage

If there's a book that you want to read that hasn't been written yet, then you must write it.

TONI MORRISON

Speakers' Bay offers the remaining authors two more weeks of finetuning their stagecraft. They review, challenge and enhance ways to maximise their workshop material, and each starts to prepare their individual keynote presentations for a final evaluation. Though they are nearly ready, they still have to reach a certain level of mastery before being given their final authority keys and sent on their way.

Bob has by this time formed some excellent friendships with some of the other authors. After working alongside one another on their respective abilities to become authorities, they have gotten to know a lot about each other's topics and their books, and have identified ways in they can collaborate in future.

They have also been able to see how far each has come. Bob finds it quite surreal to realise he's been on Authority Island six weeks.

He's taking a break on a deckchair by the pool when Jo finds him.

'Hey, Bob, how are you?'

He squints up, then quickly stands and gives her a big hug.

'Jo, it's so good to see you! Did you just get here? Where have you been?'

Jo laughs and takes the chair next to Bob's.

'I've been here mostly. But I did go back to the Social Media Cliffs of Despair for an extra week of training on some advanced YouTube and video work. I wanted to get really good at that so I can also do my own videos about my book. I'm also doing some extra work on audiobook production. So, I guess I've been around, but taking a slightly different route.'

'Well, we've clearly both come a long way since Amazon Bay then,' Bob smiles. 'How are you enjoying the journey?'

IT'S THE STORIES YOU SHARE THAT MAKE THE FACTS YOU WANT REMEMBERED PROPERLY STICKY.

'Pretty good, really. I'm more confident about speaking now I have a clearer picture in my mind about how I want to promote myself in my marketplace. I believe that video will be really important for me – more so than keynote speaking. And I'm most interested in creating online courses from my books. How was the speaker training?'

Bob fills her in on his three-week intensive, and then tells her he's one of the speakers who'll present at the next conference weekend starting in two days.

'Yes, I heard that we have to do that to earn our keys. To present keynotes as professional speakers we're going to have that extra level of confidence on stage, but also it's good to put all we've learned into real practice.' Jo screws up her face a little. 'Do you really want to do that? Be a speaker? You have other options you know.'

Bob thinks about it for a moment.

'Well yes, I think it's going to be where my biggest marketing opportunities are. Being talked about in the media, having my articles picked up by trade and business journals, and making a name for myself on the conference circuit – it'll all be a big plus for my books. I'll start writing my next one soon.'

'I'm just asking because being a speaker and getting paid for it is still risky business in my view,' Jo confides. 'Limited eyes on what you're doing, compared to thousands of eyes, when most of what you're doing is selling what you know.'

Bob listens to her carefully. She makes a good point.

'Let me ask you something though,' he says. 'What drives you to be an authority? Why are you doing all this?'

'Great question, Bob. I'm doing this to help change the world, and I want to get to as many people as I can, as fast as I can. YouTube and selling online programs are great ways to do that. Then I can also maximise my reach using social media, articles, guest blogging and podcasting, and if I have to I can still get away with a handful of speaking engagements a year. Most of what I want to do will come from my online networking and collaboration.'

Bob thinks for a minute about what Jo is saying. Is there an easier way to get his messages out to his market?

'Jo, are you saying you think that if you focus on having a great website, online presence, social media, etcetera, that you can achieve just as much as if you focus a lot more on your book?'

She nods.

'I've been doing this for a while now and have finally decided I don't care so much about my book – or even writing another one – but I *am* interested in getting my message out there as an online specialist. I realised during my file-upload that I'm just as good at making my website busy and productive as writing content for more books, so that's going to be my preferred avenue.'

'But it's the book that makes you an authority, not your online presence,' Bob frowns. 'Having a great online thing going on is fine, but the very word *authority* comes from being an author. See, *author*-ity.'

Jo senses they'll end up agreeing to disagree, but she wants to help him understand her perspective.

'Yes, you are right, Bob, but at the same time, in this day and age a really well-crafted website and online presence is enough for me. And I don't want to be a professional speaker as much as I want to be a professional blogger, vlogger and podcaster. I guess it comes down to being a recognised expert, not just an authority known for books. I'm not sure that people really care about reading books these days anyway.'

'Well, on that I must disagree,' Bob counters. 'Not everyone wants to read online, some want a lot more depth than a blog offers, and video ... Well, yes, all those things are great ways to ensure an author fully leverages their opportunities. However,

I'm certain that a book has a longer shelf life – and if it's a really good-quality book, then it can deliver someone like me a lot more leverage. For example, I can send people a copy when I'm pitching for work and still send them to my website – as you can – but the book I can autograph or sell at the back of the room.

'It still really impresses a lot of people when you are an author, and while anyone can just write any old book these days and get it to market quite quickly, doing it well is a mark of higher professionalism. Sure, a high-quality website and social media presence is good – no, *great* – for both of us, but I still think that my book will open more doors for me than what you're suggesting will work for you.'

They talk about it some more and then go looking for lunch. As they walk to the dining area, they notice a tall, very smart-looking, dark-haired woman in an expensive red suit and shiny high heels striding through the hallway. She's with another woman wearing boots, jeans and a tan-coloured jacket. They are deep in conversation. Bob and Jo both assume they are new recruits, but agree that this pair look better dressed and looking fresher than most authors they've met on the island.

The next two days of relatively quiet time pass quickly, and Bob finds himself engrossed in many conversations. The group is starting to become a serious cluster of like-minded authors who all have something unique to offer. Their specialist topics, such as leadership, marketing, communications, online media, and event management, involve skills they can see meshing well should they happen to work together in future. They are all keen to see where these business friendships might ultimately lead them.

Bob notices the tall, dark-haired woman with her sidekick several times, but never gets close enough to say hello. He is, however, quite intrigued by her. Someone has told him her name is Kris. She looks a little familiar and is obviously very sure of herself.

10

Kris the Authority

I always pretend I'm sitting across from someone.
I'm telling them a story and I don't want them to get
up until I've finished.

— JAMES PATTERSON

Kris, however, is not so much aware of being utterly sure of herself as she is aware of being very, very tired. Even with her team beside her it's been an exhausting week. Still, Kris knows that her investment of time and effort will be worth it. She just needs to keep sight of her goal.

Understanding her story means going back more than a year before her Authority Island arrival. Kris had travelled. She had gone to university – ok, she'd actually dropped out twice before finally completing her degree, but that was mostly due to boredom and lack of direction. She'd founded an excellent training business but wanted it to do even better. Her next big question was about returning to study to do an MBA. But it just didn't really feel right. She wrestled over whether to take a more formal approach to her career or take advantage of all the street smarts she'd gathered over the years.

Kris's experience had taught her that she had powerful messages and the ability to help others transform their own career paths, to help them get ahead and thrive in their own environments. The dilemma was how to best convey that and earn a great living as well.

After one long, challenging week of considering her options, she concluded it was time to investigate writing a book as opposed to taking up formal study. A friend had told her about someone who had magical abilities in the writing game, so Kris sent off an enquiry email.

The Word Witch answered her immediately with an invitation to join her in a Zoom Room the following Thursday. Kris was delighted to see that being referred by another client had saved herself an introduction fee. *Great start*, thought Kris.

Some initial research in the form of a few online straw polls and talking with other consultants had swayed her towards the idea of writing a book, but she had no idea where to really start, or what might be involved. She'd seen countless coaches write short books, race them to market and then achieve next to nothing with them, so she was determined to do her homework so that all her efforts would pay off.

A few days later, Kris logged into the Zoom Room and met Merlina. No bubbling cauldrons, no wands or warts either. In fact, she looked like a very normal, everyday person in a casual, dark-grey linen suit with a red shirt, lightly rimmed glasses framing blue eyes, and a mop of red hair that looked thoroughly untameable.

'Hey, welcome,' Merlina said, and then wasted no time in asking a long list of pointed questions.

'Why are you writing this book? Why now? Who's your audience? Are you speaking yet? How do you know they will care about your message?

Merlina challenged, thrust and parried as though in a well-rehearsed sword fight. She wanted to know everything pertinent about Kris's industry, her expertise, reasons for writing, current career level and future ambitions. Kris liked that Merlina was relaxed enough to laugh at her own jokes, but obviously had broad and deep knowledge about publishing. She offered some generalised guidance around some of Kris's ideas and sometimes probed deeper to pinpoint her motivations. By the time they had agreed to work together, Kris was thinking about her potential project on a whole new level.

She knew already that a book would only represent a part of what she wanted to achieve. Her feeling of having a *purpose* had grown exponentially in recent times, and she was absolutely sure that her success in connecting big business with small companies was due to her belief in sustainability as key to good business practice. Through her conversation with Merlina, she was starting to see an even bigger picture. Kris would focus on educating and enabling clients to do better work together. The task would be teaching them the ways of each other – getting David- and Goliath-sized companies to realise outstanding opportunities together.

Her big wake-up moment was the realisation that she could truly change the world (or at least her corner of it) and, with the right guidance and care, her journey towards becoming a top-ranking authority was going to be a lot of fun – as well, of course, as hard work. Merlina promised a rich and rewarding learning curve on her path to authority status, but assured her that it would not feel like scaling craggy mountain ranges.

The paperwork that Merlina shared with Kris at the end of their first meeting outlined their three-part plan:

1. Write a powerful, high-quality manuscript.
2. Publish that manuscript and turn it into a landmark book that will help potential clients see the value in Kris's expertise.
3. Become an authority able to master the five keys of Authority Island.

Discussing the third point on their first call together, Merlina explained that most first-time authors simply published a book and left it at that. They didn't know the secrets to getting booked for media, how speaking opportunities could be leveraged, and how all the publishing and social media platforms – some Kris had never even heard of – worked for them. But Merlina and her team were going to make her savvy in all the areas that mattered and help her avoid the ones that didn't.

It was going to be a year-long (or longer) project, and Kris was going to learn and evolve a lot in that time.

Using Merlina's well-developed processes made the writing easy and Kris's manuscript came together quickly. Once the first draft was done, they worked together to refine it. When it was ready for what Merlina called the test-pilot phase, Kris asked a few industry friends and a client or two to let her know if the book had value, and to identify what still needed to be added. She waited impatiently for feedback, then did some rewriting.

Finally, the manuscript was ready to be sent to an editor. Merlina explained that the editor's role was to push the manuscript to a superior level – and she was right. The resulting questions, corrections, thought-provoking feedback, and, in some areas, radical alterations, made the manuscript feel as though, before a baby bird, all its feathers had suddenly come in. Soon it would be ready to fly the nest.

Formatting the manuscript and perfecting the book's design also needed to be done carefully as it needed to incorporate branding that Kris had already invested in. As that started to evolve further, she and Merlina discussed subtle ways they could enhance that branding and really develop her social media and website further.

As the book started to take shape, Merlina instructed Kris on what would happen next.

'You see, writing and publishing a book is only part of your journey as an authority. There's so much more. Many people fall over along the way, but you're working with me and my team, and we haven't lost an author yet. So, strap on your life jacket, honey. We're going sailing.'

Kris was never quite sure how serious Merlina was when she started talking about sailing. But by now she was starting to see her book coming to life, and it was looking fantastic. Not only that, her awareness of just how much she didn't know about some parts of what lay ahead was expanding, and she was fully involved in the project now. *And loving it.*

She started paying attention to things Merlina deemed important – such as how conference speakers were either really good or really boring and what made the difference.

'Is it their ability to tell stories, and engage an audience?'

'Yes, that's exactly it,' Merlina beamed at her. 'You see, stories make the facts sticky so they lodge in listeners' minds and they *remember* them. That's the way to get facts into their heads and stay there, but telling a good and relevant story takes practice. Learning new platform skills doesn't happen overnight and there's a huge difference between someone who can just do public speaking and someone who can inspire audiences to take action. It's the same with writing. Only the best can spur readers to make changes, start a movement, or develop a new way of thinking.

'Anyone can learn this stuff, but a level of mastery is required if you're going to really own your stage – and own your subject. By the time we're ready to go sailing, my dear, I want you to be ready to own your subject. So, let's get busy.'

They had just sent the nearly completed book files off to a group of reviewers: industry professionals, authors, and consultants in complementary business fields. Their testimonials were going to take a few weeks to come in, so Merlina and Kris got busy learning a few *non*-author authority skills.

The Word Witch team took Kris's middling competence on stage to the level of someone whose powerful presence who could command her audience, inspire them to buy her book and see her as a highly competent, potential solution to their business issues.

Kris learned about setting fees, staying calm in the face of wardrobe or technical malfunctions, and sticking to agreed speaking timeslots. Chapters were wrangled into content for workbooks, audiobooks, ebooks and condensed versions for giveaways. She also mastered being ready for media inquiries, set up her social media and webinar masterclass options for boosting traffic to her inquiry funnels, and developed some of her book material into derivative products.

Eight months had flown by and her head was buzzing – but in a good way – when Merlina called and asked if she was ready for their trip.

'Trip? What trip?' Kris asked.

'Why, to Authority Island, of course! Remember it's in our contract? It's time to publish your book and launch it – and you – out into the world. You can both fly free and do what you're here to do.'

Merlina chuckled – a deep, warm sound that Kris found always gave her a feeling of confidence and surety. So far, everything had been taken care of, and her learning curve had indeed been steady – not a craggy mountain range at all.

'Ok then,' Kris hesitated. 'Is it a *real* island?' She was so used to Merlina's metaphors by then that she still wasn't really sure.

Lowering her voice, Merlina said, 'Yes Kris, it's a real island – and we can only get there by boat. You're so well-prepared for this. It's going to be easy for you to pick up each of the five keys you need to take to the gatekeeper to receive your own gold authority key.'

A thousand questions were crashing around in Kris's mind, like butterflies in a windstorm. Before she could ask any, Merlina wrapped up the call saying that she'd explain the rest on the way to the island.

'Meet me at the marina at 8am tomorrow. Pack a bag. We'll be staying for about 10 days.'

And with that, she was gone.

11

Time to Set Sail

'The truth is, you could write a masterpiece, but if you're hiding it under a rock, no-one will ever know.'

— BETHANY ATAZADEH

When Kris arrives at the marina, Merlina is talking with what looks to be their skipper, supplies already loaded onto a sleek 56-foot yacht. It looks sturdy enough to take them a reasonable distance and Kris wonders just how far away the island is. Merlina calls out a happy hello, and soon they're standing on the gently rocking deck. Kris smiles up at the unfurling sails and gives a small thanks to the book angels, who have provided beautiful weather for their trip.

Sailing through the day, Kris and Merlina talk for hours until finally the island looms ahead. Kris is a little jittery as they drop anchor, and the skipper helps her down into a dinghy for the final 300-meter run into the beach. Merlina pre-warned Kris that she has an assistant on the island, and they can see him waiting on the sand.

'Nick, meet Kris,' Merlina says as they step onshore.

Kris extends her hand, but Nick surprises her with a brief, bold bear hug instead.

'In our tribe here, just a handshake will never do', he says with a smile. He is a lean, tall, good-looking man, with warm, brown eyes, and slightly greying eyebrows to match the very short, once jet-black hair on his head. He picks up their bags and they follow him up a path behind a fringe of palm trees to a cottage with a wide verandah and shuttered windows. This, Kris already knows, is where they'll stay as she takes the steps necessary to collect the first few keys that she requires to unlock the Authority Gate.

First, she'll need to get her website and social media keys by having her platforms checked and evaluated. Next, she'll achieve successful uploads to the publishing platforms she and Merlina have already identified. From there, she'll have a short stay at Speakers' Bay and likely no more than one day at the Publicity Forest, before making the final trek to the Authority Gate. Kris has been assured that all the work she's already done will help her work her way around the island quickly. Plus, she's got Merlina and Nick to call on for advice.

With an early night in mind, they call up a light supper and a splendid bottle of New Zealand merlot.

'What are those other buildings over there behind the trees?', Kris asks as she finishes dessert.

'That is where you don't really want to be,' Nick replies with a wink at Merlina. 'They're the Thinking Huts. It's the place for authors who think they can just turn up and publish, imagining that it will give them automatic authority as authors. What they soon realise is that there are a number of additional steps to go through to really earn that authority.'

Merlina adds, 'The authors do manage to who get past the first few stages are often quite successful, but it takes a lot of trial and error, and for some the learning curve is a bit like ...'

'A craggy range of mountains!' Kris finishes the sentence for her. 'Ahh, ok. I get it.'

'Kris, all the work my team and I have been doing *with* you, parts of it *for* you, means you can fast track some of your authority journey. You've still had to roll up your sleeves and learn a lot of new skills, but we've been able to guide you past many of the typical distractions – all the time-wasting exercises and bright, shiny objects that many authors get sidelined by.'

'She's right,' Nick agrees. 'We see a lot of authors come and go here, and most are exhausted and broke by the time they depart for the mainland. The costs of trial and error are huge in this game, and there's never any guarantee of success or even a return on their investment.'

Nick pauses, then looks at Merlina as though checking to see if he can press on. She nods.

'Kris, there is no guarantee of you having any success either, you know. Despite all your training, having excellent files and a high-quality book with lots of potential leverage, you still have a lot of work to do to really get the most out of your investment. The goal is to achieve a state of what we call 'fully realised leverage'.

'As you become even more comfortable and confident as an authority, you'll notice more opportunities will come your way. But to score better speaking gigs, charge higher fees and become a highly sought-after expert – for media and prospective clients – you'll need to keep on producing fresh content and keep on top of your area of authority. This is a much bigger commitment to your career than just writing a book. Are you ready for that?'

Kris only has to think about his question for a heartbeat. She drains her glass and puts it down firmly on the table.

Looking at Nick and Merlina directly, she declares, 'You bet!'

'Right then, Kris, best we get to bed,' says Merlina. 'We've a special guide calling first thing in the morning to escort us up that huge hill over there.'

12

The View from Above

'Substitute "damn" every time you're inclined to write "very". Your editor will delete it and the writing will be just as it should be.'

— MARK TWAIN

Naturally, it's an easy morning ascent up to the Website Mountain lookout because Merlina has already built up and refined Kris's site. They have more than enough time for a good look at the view of the whole island. Merlina points out the tent flags fluttering in the breeze far below at the Social Media Cliffs of Despair.

'We'll be going there tomorrow. It'll be a harder day than today, but I'm confident you'll be fine.'

'Why are they called the Social Media Cliffs of Despair?' asks Kris.

'Because many people are frustrated by the never-ending parts of getting your social media presence set up and working well. It's a constant and necessary learning curve with many new moving parts popping up all the time,' Merlina smiles. 'More than a few people joke about jumping off the cliffs instead of continuing to master that area.'

'Oh ...'

'But you'll be ok! We've already got your Facebook, Twitter, Instagram and LinkedIn set up properly, Nick is checking and finetuning your YouTube channel as we speak, and your videos and podcasts were already excellent when we met. You'll breeze through, I'm sure.'

She turns to the other side of the island and points out the Publishing Bays along the northern shore.

'That area's already just about taken care of too, though there's still some basic information to take in around that side of things. But I have a very special surprise for you later today, so let's make a move, shall we?'

Back at the cottage, the surprise turns out to be a young man named Alex. He is a little scruffy looking, with a scraggly beard and a mop of unruly blonde curls, and a very serious expression that occasionally transforms into a youthful grin. Alex paces with excitement, gesticulating with big hands as he shares a brilliant marketing strategy. His recommendations for a social media campaign and publicity for her book launch sounded very effective, yet entirely manageable – a great combination of simplicity and cunning.

'Kris,' Merlina interrupts gently. 'You don't need to keep making all those notes, because Alex will be coming with us for the rest of our journey on the island.'

'Oh, ok! That's great.'

'And then, Alex will return to the mainland with us so you can continue to work with him when you need his specialist services.'

'Oh, wow – that's fantastic!' Kris is overwhelmed. 'What a good idea.'

Clearly, young Alex is perfect for the role, and Merlina explains that he is trained to give her the right kind of help when she needs it.

'Part of what we do is find ways to ensure you don't have to be expert at everything yourself,' Merlina continues. 'But having someone like Alex on board means your opportunities are always maximised. That way you get to do what you do best, and everyone wins. My team will also continue to support you with whatever you need for the next few months, and even beyond that if you wish. Especially as you are already starting to think about your next book, aren't you?'

Kris is close to tears with gratitude. Everything she's longed for is within reach, and she has a dynamic team behind her. What can possibly go wrong?

The next few days pass by in a blur as they work through the challenges of social media, and upload her manuscript to Amazon and IngramSpark. Because she has the right files on hand, the uploads are super easy, and Alex takes care of keyword searches, descriptions, and linking her publishing platforms with her website and social media accounts. Kris is ready to launch.

Their arrival at Speakers' Bay is quiet, and Kris is nervous as she walks into the convention centre to make her presentation. It's time for her keynote on the topic of her book. This final assessment should win her a key at Speakers' Bay. She looks at no-one on the way, not wanting to risk any distractions. There is far too much riding on the outcome. Kris is only days away from reaching the Authority Gate, and she's determined to make it, then return home and get busy building her career as a highly paid, highly sought-after consultant, speaker and author.

Bob sits in the same place that he took when he first arrived at the Speakers' Bay convention centre. This time though, he's a much better judge of the quality of the presenters he is about to hear and will really understand what makes them good, great or a general waste of his time. He is himself listed to speak the next morning and hopes he's as prepared as he thinks he is, because he's sure as heck ready to go home.

The lights dim and the MC introduces the next speaker. Bob's not heard of her before, but he's intrigued by her branding – Kris McQueen, Curator of David and Goliath Business Relationships.

The speaker who walks on stage is the dark-haired woman he saw earlier, the one with stunning style and carefree confidence. He leans forward a little and mentally blots out all other distractions in the room.

She starts with a story about someone launching a small company, and someone else running a bigger one, but she makes it sound like a pitch for a Hollywood movie. It's a romance, a love story, a saga of adversity and overcoming the odds to end up at the altar of commitment in order to forge a business relationship that might not have worked out otherwise. Above all, it's a tale of triumph.

Bob is swept up in the story, and the speaker's points hit like cupid's arrows. He can feel her passion for her story and finds he has real empathy for the heroes she portrays. He thinks back to Abraham, the speaker who first inspired him several weeks earlier, and compares him with this woman, Kris. Her delivery style is different, but in so many ways it is just as good.

Yes, there are good speakers and great ones. But where does he fit on the scale? Can he become as good as them? He hopes so.

Kris earns a standing ovation. As she takes in the rowdy applause, she feels that everything she's been working so hard for – the last piece of the puzzle – is falling into place. She is primed, she is ready, and there is no doubt in her mind that she fully deserves that final authority key.

Tomorrow she has only to traverse the last few miles of the island to reach the Authority Gate.

13

Bright, Shiny Objects

Kris meets with Alex and Merlina the next morning, packed and ready to leave straight after breakfast. She's surprised to see them both relaxing over coffee and showing no signs of the impatience she is feeling about the final leg of the journey.

'Oh, well no, that's because we have to wait here,' Merlina says quite casually.

Kris is quite disconcerted. The stress of the last few days, suppressed momentarily by her relief at having delivered a fantastic presentation, returns with a vengeance, threatening to erupt like Vesuvius.

'What do you mean you're not coming? Of course, you're coming – both of you! Why ever not?' she implores, fighting hard against the tears of frustration that are unexpectedly brewing.

Kris suddenly has a vision of herself doing what was previously unthinkable: crawling to the Authority Gate and stopping just short of the finish line – just as she has done on other occasions in her life.

Alex is clearly uncomfortable as he picks up his cup and practically hides behind it, while Merlina looks somewhat sternly at Kris and sighs. It is often this way at the end of the journey.

Authors get scared and think maybe they've been wrong to even imagine getting to this point. Going on alone to the end is sometimes totally unfathomable to them, which is why she hesitates to let them know in advance. Better to not let their anxiety grow ahead of what is really only a momentary parting of ways.

'Kris, you've got this,' Merlina consoles. 'You don't need me, or Alex. You are ready to do this and it's amazing you've got all your keys so far. But this level of authority, it's *yours* – not mine, not anyone else's. It's yours and yours alone. And that is why you have to present your keys to the gatekeeper alone.'

She smiles warmly at her protégé and tries to convey that she really does believe in Kris's ability to make it on her own.

'But what if I lose my way? There's still several miles to go, and I have all this luggage, and ...' Kris realises it all sounds pretty lame, even to her ears.

'Leave your luggage here. We'll be meeting you back at the cottage,' Merlina counters. 'All you have to do is cross the final valley, go around the bend and keep walking straight. You'll see the signs, and you'll be ok – seriously. Like I said, *you've got this!*

'Now, get yourself a quick cup of coffee and eat something. You need to leave in under 30 minutes – and don't forget to pack a lunch. We'll meet you at the front door. Come along, Alex!'

Merlina and Alex sweep out of the room, leaving Kris struggling to down a cup of coffee. Eating is unlikely – her stomach is doing flips.

Twenty-five minutes later, Kris, Merlina and Alex meet at the front door of the complex. Unsure of how she is to travel, but knowing some walking is required, Kris has done a quick change, grabbing jeans and hiking boots from her luggage. The five precious keys are stuffed into the bottom of her red-leather cross-body bag. She is somewhat out of breath at the speed with which she's gotten here, but having less time to think about the day ahead is probably for the best.

She says her goodbyes and sets out for what she hopes will be a relatively short and easy final stage.

The terrain through a low valley is easy walking for the first hour. She occasionally meets friendly people coming back the other way, and they briefly stop and talk. Most want to know about her book and to congratulate her on reaching this stage of the authority journey. Some offer what seems like smart advice about additional things she might like to write about one day, or ways she could further develop parts of her area of expertise. While she's grateful, she almost wishes they'd leave her alone. Everyone seems to have a vested interest in how she can keep doing better and better.

By lunchtime she's getting hungry. She'd forgotten to pack a lunch despite Merlina's her that morning, and she's long since finished the bottle of water Alex handed her as she left. Another person walks towards her now and Kris can see he's carrying armfuls of pizza boxes. She thinks it odd, but she's pleased when he gives her a cheery wave.

'*Ciao*,' he says. 'My name is Pietro and I am here to ensure you have some lunch. You still have a few more miles to go and most people forget to bring food. I can offer you two different flavours of pizza my mama made: pepperoni or margherita. They are still warm, so please, choose.'

'Pietro, thank you! It's so good to see you. I'll have a margherita pizza, *grazie mille*. I'm so hungry and it smells so good!'

Spotting a grassy knoll close to the path, she sits down and starts to eat, doubly delighted when Pietro offers her a cold bottle of water.

'Thank you!'

'You are very welcome, *signora*. I will wait and take the box away when you're finished. Eh, *signora* you must have worked hard to get here. So, tell me about your book, eh?'

Between bites, Kris starts to explain her story, her passion for David-and-Goliath business relationships, and how she wants to help people do better business together.

Pietro asks a few questions every now and then. And then he poses one that stops her cold.

'So, *signora*, that all sounds pretty good, but don't you see that you've clearly missed a big part of what you're talking about in your book?'

Kris frowns as she opens her mouth to say 'No', but she's stopped by the great, sudden uncertainty that maybe he's right. Might he be onto something? The more she tries to think about the question, the more terrified she becomes. If there's a problem she's missed that is obvious to this pizza man, then can she really be so confident about her book?

'Please, tell me what you think it is.' Kris doesn't really want to ask, but she's so stuck in her own head that she can't think beyond her confusion.

'*Signora*, really, it's very obvious, isn't it?'

'No, it's *not*!' she wants to scream it at him, to cry even. This uncertainty is unbearable. Has she messed up? If so, how?

Instead, she simply says calmly, 'No, I'm sorry, I don't see it.'

Pietro smiles and says, 'If managers don't know how to speak the different languages of each other's companies, then the relationship is never going to be easy. People need to learn each other's jargon to be able to communicate.'

The icy feeling that started creeping over her a few moments earlier hits her like a tsunami. She has completely overlooked the issues of communication and language barriers. And if this man can see that already, then what are her readers going to think? How can she possibly sell her authority when there's such a devastating gap in her book?

She barely notices Pietro leaving with his pizza boxes. The realisation of her terrible omission leaves her so depressed that she's still sitting by the path when another man approaches.

'Hi, are you ok?'

Kris looks bleakly up at him. She thinks she recognises him from the Speakers' Bay convention centre, but she's not quite sure.

'Um, ah, yes, thank you.' She doesn't feel certain though and can hear how unconvincing she sounds.

He sits down beside her and waits for a full minute before speaking.

'My name is Bob, and I'm on my way to the Authority Gate. I saw you speak yesterday at the conference – you were outstanding. I was so taken with your story and your ability to share it. I have to say, I stopped and rethought my entire readiness for this last stage of my journey after seeing you in action.'

Kris stays quiet, still thinking about her own issues.

Bob goes on, 'I know that this is a strange journey, but it seems like we're going the same way, so maybe you'd like to share the road for a while?'

Finally, Kris rouses herself.

'I'm glad you liked my speech,' she says. 'Did you have to present too?'

'Yes, I was brought forward to last thing yesterday, so I was able to start the final trek today. I've noticed they seem to stagger the departures so that we all don't walk together, so I'm surprised to see you here. Are you ok?'

'Um, well, sort of ... I just ... Well, I'm having a moment of panic about my book and feel like I've missed something vitally important. Now ... Well, I'm feeling a bit silly, and not sure if I should turn back and talk about it with my coach.'

Bob looks at her in astonishment.

'Really?'

'Yes, really.'

'But your presentation yesterday was brilliant. Everything you said made perfect sense and you totally owned the stage as you delivered it,' Bob says. 'Plus, you're clearly very confident in your branding and ... Well, I just don't believe it.'

'Yes, but this piece I've overlooked *might* be vitally important. How can I go through the final publishing phase and not address it? I really think I need to rewrite a whole section.'

IMPOSTER SYNDROME SEEMS TO BE A VERY PERSISTENT FIEND IN THE WORLD OF AUTHORS, CREATIVES, AND TALENTED EXPERTS. GIVE IT THE OLD HEAVE-HO AS SOON AS IT SHOWS UP AND REMEMBER TO BE WHO YOU ARE: A NECESSARY CONDUIT OF POWERFUL INFORMATION THAT MIGHT CHANGE SOMEONE'S WORLD.

Bob shreds a long piece of grass he's been playing with, curls it up into a tiny ball and flicks it away. Finally, he turns and looks at Kris.

'Seriously – if you feel that way, go right ahead, but it sounds to me like you have other choices. One, write a second book or an updated edition; or two, well, there is no number two, I made that up. You would be mad to re-do it now rather than simply update it later or write a follow-up book. Look how far you've made it on this journey already. You have the five mastery keys and the Authority Gate is just another mile or so up the road!

'You know,' he says, 'it sounds to me like you've talked too long to the Bright Shiny Object tramps who litter this pathway.'

'The who?'

'They're known as the BSOs. And it's their *job* to distract us. That's why we have to walk this last part of the journey alone, so we really do totally own our topic and are committed to our authority by the time we reach the gate.'

Kris's mouth drops open as she takes this in. She thinks about the pizza guy and all the other enthusiastic people she's met on the path that day. Yes, she now sees exactly what they were doing. They were all coaxing her to rethink everything she has so far believed about her authority and her book. They were there to challenge her own feelings of success.

'Well, I never,' she says incredulously. 'That's so sneaky! And I nearly fell for it!'

Bob smiles and stands up. Holding out his hand to help her to her feet, he laughs as she swears, 'Dammit! How did you know?'

'I've learned a lot since I've been here. You see, I turned up convinced I was already equipped to publish and promote my book, but soon figured out I knew very little. At every point on the island, I've had to learn and discover more to earn each of my keys. Along the way I met people who had been through the entire journey, got their keys, and then got stuck like you nearly did today. One of them was here for the second time. He'd turned back, but when he got home and thought about it all he realised that he should have simply kept going and not fallen for the BSOs. It's that second-guessing that is always going to stop people like us. Some also call it "imposter syndrome".'

'Yes, I've definitely heard of that,' says Kris.

'So how have you managed to gather your mastery keys and not learn about this other stuff?'

Kris tells him about how she had Merlina and her team of experts alongside her from when she first started on her book. She explains the processes that made it easy to write, so that by the time she arrived on Authority Island she was really well-prepared, with reviews sorted and files correctly formatted, to publish and promote her book.

Bob is astounded that such a service exists. He explains his lengthy and steep learning curve, and she says it sounds to her more like a craggy mountain range than a curve. Bob laughs and agrees.

They turn a corner then, and the path suddenly widens. The dirt and rocky terrain give way to bricks and tidy hedges on either side.

Up ahead they can see a shiny marble wall with a golden gate glimmering in the sun. An old man waits there, dressed in gold robe. He walks barefoot towards them, and asks that they proceed the rest of the way one at a time.

'Well, I guess this is where we part company, for now at least,' Bob says as he gives Kris his business card. 'Look me up when we're back on the mainland, so we can keep talking.'

'I'd love to.' Kris hands hers over to Bob, and they start to shake hands, but Kris leans in and wraps her arms around him instead. 'Members of the same tribe hug, and I think we'll be both be in this tribe for a while yet. We'll see each other on stages and in bookstores, and no doubt there's potential for us to write together sometime. So yes, let's keep in touch.'

'Done!' Bob tucks Kris's card into his pocket and waits for her to go ahead. 'You go first. You were going to get here ahead of me anyway.'

'Thanks, Bob!'

With that, Kris turns to follow the old man. When they reach the gate, he holds out his hand. She passes over her five keys and in return he drops into her palm a single heavy gold key with her name engraved on it.

'This is your reward,' he says, 'for investing in yourself and wanting to share your wisdom with the world – to make change and help others to grow. The journey you have been on since starting your book and coming to this island has been about helping you to understand all the parts of becoming not just someone who wrote a good book, but also an authority able to promote yourself to your market, using your book and all the other tools at your disposal.

'Keep this key on your desk to remind you that you have earned the right to stand boldly as an authority among others who also have learned the value of their own experience and wisdom and how to share that.'

The old man smiles, showing beautiful straight teeth, and ushers her through the Authority Gate: 'Bye-bye!'

As Kris walks between the gateposts clutching her authority key, she feels a huge surge of confidence and knows for certain that there'll be no holding her back now from stepping into the role she has wanted for so long – that of being a world-class authority in her field.

The next thing she knows, she's standing on the verandah of the cottage on the beach, laughing and celebrating with Merlina and Alex. It's time to go back to the mainland, get busy on her next book, and take up all the opportunities that are opening up to her.

After Bob has been given his own gold authority key and the 'bye-bye' farewell, he hesitates before entering the gateway.

He'd been so clear in advising Kris, but he still has moments of doubt about his own ability to call himself an authority. Sure, his book is well-crafted, he knows how to promote it and himself, but will anyone really want to hear what he has to say?

He looks at the old man, who is standing expectantly, radiating encouragement, and feels an unexpected rush of pride in the person he's become over the past few weeks. Yes, he trusts his topic and abilities, and his journey forward will be better for all that he has learned.

With a deep breath, he smiles his thanks at the old man and steps through the gate, clutching his key.

The next day, Bob and Kris meet again on the beach, joining a jostling group of authors all waiting to go to their respective boats moored out by the reef. A hum rises as they talk and joke about their triumphs and failures. Bob waves to Jo in the crowd and pulls Kris over to meet her. He's sure they'll have lots in common.

Some of the authors are excited about what lies ahead. Others look rather downcast. They simply wait, listening to the conversation all around.

A quiet woman taps Merlina on the shoulder.

'Excuse me,' she says. 'My name's Sue.'

She waves at the hubbub all around.

'I came here hoping I could write and publish a great book, but listening to everyone made me realise I still have such a long way to go. I hear you're good at helping people like me …' she trails off.

'Great to meet you, Sue! I'd be happy to talk. Once we're back on the mainland, do give me a call.'

Merlina delves into her bag and pulls out a business card. Sue shakes Merlina's hand, smiling shyly as she takes the card and puts it in her pocket.

In Summary

Say what you say, write what you mean, make a photograph in the mind of the reader

— STEPHEN KING

Lots of authors start out like our three heroes. There's so much information available on the internet about writing books and publishing them that most people think it's really easy. But as outlined in this parable, though things might go smoothly, there are myriad chances for to get derailed along the way.

Sue is a great example of so many authors who think writing a book is easy, but then find it's really not. That's because the real work begins after you finish the writing – and it is there that many come unstuck and simply give up. Authors like Sue might end up with one or two books, but they typically fail to gain real traction when it comes to being an authority who commands respect and attention from those they wish to impress with their expertise.

Bob's story is typical of most authors with some degree of industry expertise and experience in professional speaking and training. Though they think they have a real edge on their competitors, their learning curve is very expensive – and won't become apparent until after they finish writing.

Kris, in comparison, had the help of the dynamic team at Indie Experts, who guide authorities-to-be like her through the many pitfalls of writing, editing, production, reviews, and the platforms their books are published on. They then work with authors in the year after production and publishing – and beyond, if they require it – as the journey doesn't end when you hit 'publish'. They ensure that, like Kris, their authors know what to do with their book after it's published.

It comes down to this: many non-fiction authors fail to understand that there's a difference between being an author and being an authority. It's all about leverage. How much leverage do you want to get out of writing a book in the first place?

It's rather like setting out on a car trip. You get in, look at the needle on the tank and turn the key. The journey is full of potential – you can go as far and as fast as you want, depending on your engine and what petrol you put into it.

Many authors self-publish for the first time and end up with what I call 'localised leverage'. After a few months there are still very few sales or reviews and certainly not much influence to be seen. And influence is one of the primary desires for writing a book: influence and recognition. You know you're stuck in the localised-leverage zone when it feels like hard work to gain sales traction, it's dawning on you that there are few points of difference between your book and others, and it's even hard sometimes to persuade people to take a free copy. After a while, it feels like it was more a waste of time and effort than something you're really proud of.

Some authors self-publish a book and get it to work for them as a promising marketing tool, thus reaching a point where they have a lot of potential leverage. Getting speaking and consulting work is easier then, but they are constantly on a busy treadmill where the learning curve really seems more like a craggy mountain range than a smooth trajectory. You know you're in this place when you end up giving away a lot more time and books than you get paid for. Maybe you still don't feel that you own your position as an expert yet and you're still making up your mind about being the ruler of that particular topic. You might still occasionally consider getting a 'real job' or tell yourself that your book and some speaking work is really your semi-retirement thing.

But all the way over in the red zone is where you become a fully leveraged authority. Here's where the cool kids with the fast cars hang out. Here's where you get to enjoy being highly sought-after for advice on your area of expertise. You're the one the media calls for comment when your topic is in the news. Your dance card is full – with a waiting list. People want to do business with you. You know you've fully leverage your authority when you are doing the work you love to do with the clients you love to work with. And you're earning top-dollar for your wisdom and expertise.

To be a fully leveraged authority, you need to have mastered the five points of authority.

1. **PUBLISHING PLATFORMS:** you get your book to your readers easily.

2. **ONLINE PRESENCE:** your website, and social media are working for you.

3. **PROFILE HIGHLIGHTS AND BRANDING:** your brand works hard for you, and you're winning awards, getting great reviews and more.

4. **PUBLICITY AND PROMOTION:** the media call you when they need an expert – and you know how to respond and perform in that interview.

5. **PRESENTING:** you're great at it and you own the stages you stand on.

One of the best things about being a fully leveraged authority is that when you get there, the title is 'SIR' –because you will have *security*, *influence* and *recognition*. With localised or even potential leverage you might have some influence, maybe even some security in your ability to be paid for your expertise, but to get that recognition you'll need to become a fully leveraged authority. As one of my favourite authorities, Keith Abraham, says: 'You can't just *go* there, till you *grow* there'.

IN SUMMARY

In order to fully extend yourself from authorship to authority, working with a publishing team (including a coach or mentor) who understand the entire journey is an excellent way to minimise your risk and reduce the incline on your learning curves. You'll need to think about all that goes into your journey, before, during, *and* after you write a great book.

Acknowledgements

Very special thanks to Ann Dettori Wilson for her humour, expertise, encouragement and review of this book. When we started Indie Experts together, I don't think either of us quite expected to have as much fun with our publishing business as we do.

Thanks to all my reviewers and beta readers, Kathy Rees, Sue Adstrum, Bronwyn Reid, Brad Hauck, Lindsay Adams, Alexander Carlton, for your suggestions, ideas, inspiration, and encouragement.

Thank you to the extraordinary Keith Abraham from whom I've continued to learn from and look up to for many years now. When I first saw him on stage as a professional speaker he talked about how you can't Go there till you Grow there in the same way Abraham did in this story and that's stayed with me for a very long time now.

To Steve Lowell who sparked the early inspiration for the story and to Steve and Jayne for keeping that inspiration burning bright these last few months as the story evolved and came to wrap itself around all my work as a global publishing coach and professional speaker. To Mindy Gibbins-Klein, David Pisarra, Adam Houlihan, and Ian Stephens for your extraordinary reviews and generous feedback. Thank you.

To Chris Wildeboar and Tanya McQueen, thanks for your names and the extra input you've both had into my ability to work at my best creative levels in 2020. To Lindsey Dawson – once again I learned so much from your editing and feedback ... it's been delightful to reconnect over our shared passion for books again in 2020.

Thanks for the images Penny Hauck – you have such an amazing creative future.

Finally, to Lauren, Daniela, and Renée for simply outstanding work as part of my magic production team – the Vavavoom in my magic wand once again. Thank you.

 ANN DETTORI WILSON has been exercising her abilities to create outstanding books for hundreds of authors since taking over specialist typesetting company, Post Pre-press, servicing the traditional publishing industry operators in 2008. Since then she has gone on to create Independent Ink in 2015, and cofounded Indie Experts in 2019 with Dixie Maria Carlton.

Recognised throughout Australasia for her exemplary skills in helping authors produce their best books possible, and for her unique position that encompasses both traditional and self-publishing services, she is also regularly invited as a judge of book awards. Ann sits on the Queensland Writers Centre board, and is herself the best selling author of *The Entrepreneurs Guide to Self-Publishing*.

DIXIE MARIA CARLTON started up one of the first Collaborative Publishing companies in Australasia in 2006, while also forging her career as a specialist business and marketing coach and professional speaker. Pubishing quickly took over her life, and hundreds of authors and books later, she met up with Ann Dettori Wilson and they created Indie Experts Pty Ltd in 2019.

Dixie's specialist areas as a publishing coach, and experts industry coach have blended all her passions of marketing, business, speaking, and writing perfectly. She is a prolific writer, fierce advocate for telling great stories, and still speaks when invited to anyone wanting to understand more about the authors' journey towards becoming an authority.

IF YOU'RE NEED A GUIDE FOR YOUR OWN AUTHORITY JOURNEY ...

If you are even just thinking about how a book could help your business or assist in building your brand, now is the best time to talk with Indie Experts about what you have in mind, and why. We are used to working with expectations like Sue's, Bob's and Kris's, and have helped authors from all corners of the globe to develop excellent manuscripts, produce high-quality books and then publish them to achieve extraordinary outcomes. Wherever you are on your authority journey, we have options to help you reach your desired destinations with reduced learning curves, easy travel options, and both economy and first class cabins available.

CHECK OUT OUR ONLINE PROGRAMS:

First Think, Plan and Write Your Book
The Ten Steps to Becoming an Author
Educating, Exposing and Extending Authors of Non-Fiction

Visit www.indieexperts.com.au/authority-authors and use the code AUTHOR1TY1SLAND on any of our programs for extra bonus content to help you plan your authority journey.

www.indieexperts.com.au

Facebook @indieexperts
Twitter @indieexperts
Instagram @indieexperts
LinkedIn @indieexperts

www.ingramcontent.com/pod-product-compliance
Lightning Source LLC
Chambersburg PA
CBHW050320010526
44107CB00055B/2319